THE ANXIE

COMFORT &
ENCOURAGEMENT
JOURNAL

Gentle prompts and exercises for letting
go and finding inner peace

Maybe you find yourself worrying about all the unknown variables on your daily to-do list. Or maybe you're living with Anxiety Disorder, in which case you've probably had more than your share of racing thoughts, shortness of breath, an inability to focus or concentrate on the things that actually deserve your attention, and a plethora of other not-so-fun symptoms. But there's hope. And where there's hope, there's space for calm and joy. And vice versa.

This journal is designed to help you cultivate habits of gentle, comforting and sometimes humorous self-care. By taking the time to regularly ground yourself in the moment, you can help calm those anxious, intrusive thoughts and bring your focus back to what matters most: finding peace of mind. Pay attention to your feelings and ask yourself, how can I best meet my needs in this moment? Water? Rest? Validation? Comfort?

BE KIND TO YOURSELF.

Remember that facing your anxiety is a process. There's no right or wrong way, so do what works for you.

TAKE IT DAY BY DAY.

Hopefully the activities and exercises that follow will help bring you a little closer to calm, a little nearer to joy, a little snugglier with a snuggly feeling. After all, a little goes a long way.

WE'RE ALL IN THIS TOGETHER.

Nancy Hoffman

FOUNDER/EDITOR-IN-CHIEF
Sweatpants & Coffee

A new week is
a new chance

to be the person my
coffee thinks I can be.

It's not likely, but there's
always a chance.

Write down four positive statements about yourself.
This can be very difficult for Anxiety Blobs.
Pretend you are a kindly observer in your life.
Here's one to start you off:

"I DO THINGS THAT ARE DIFFICULT!"

1 _____
_____

_____

2 _____
_____

_____

3 _____
_____

_____

4 _____
_____

_____

WHAT DO YOU WISH PEOPLE KNEW ABOUT YOU?

The real, deep-down you? It can be scary to open up,
but you can start right now by acknowledging
your hidden self on these pages.

Go outside as soon as you can and look up at the clouds.
(When was the last time you did that?)
Watch them for a few minutes or as long as you like.
What shapes do you see? Draw and write about them here.

Think back to a day when you had little to no anxiety.
Remember how that felt. What was it like?
What can you take from that experience?
If you can't think of anything, that's okay.
Describe the scene in as much detail as you
can recall and see where that takes you.

When I make the conscious decision to accept myself as I am in the moment, I:

* am less judgmental of myself and others

* can respond to the world from a place of kindness

* remember I am worthy of goodness

* am more grateful

* like the goofy, imperfect, magical unicorn that I am

* have the emotional space to figure out what I need

* take responsibility for my own happiness

* gently release myself from unrealistic expectations

* celebrate every wobbly step forward (or backward or sideways, if that's what I need to do)

How do you feel?

Doodle whatever animal you most feel like today. Whatever your stripes (or scales, or fins), you've got this.

Set a timer for 10 minutes and find a comfy, quiet spot to sit. Rather than try to name specific thoughts or concerns running through your mind today, see if you can spot an overall theme in your feelings. There are no wrong answers. What comes to the surface? What do you make of it?

Read all of the words on this page out loud in a low, angry voice.

gazebo * flamingo * spatula * ephemeral
* butterfly * coconut * mellifluous *
bungalow * kumquat * bric-a-brac *
diphthong * pumpernickel * squeegee
* kangaroo * effervescent * waddle
* lackadaisical * hullabaloo * cucumber
* lollygagging * pumpkin * skedaddle *
cerulean * malarkey * snickerdoodle
* underpants * hollow * bombastic
* fandango * bamboozle

DID YOU MAKE IT ALL THE WAY THROUGH
WHILE KEEPING A STRAIGHT FACE?

WRITE DOWN AN ANXIOUS THOUGHT ON YOUR MIND TODAY.

_____

_____

NOW CHECK OFF IF YOU:

O had more than six hours of sleep

O drank water

O ate food

O **BONUS** ate fruits and vegetables

O got fresh air

O went for a walk

O took meds

O talked to a friend

O took vitamins/supplements

O listened to music

O took a shower or bath

Now go take care of yourself, Anxiety Blob.

Fill in this map with three obstacles you've already overcome and one you have yet to finish, then draw yourself emerging victorious at the end.

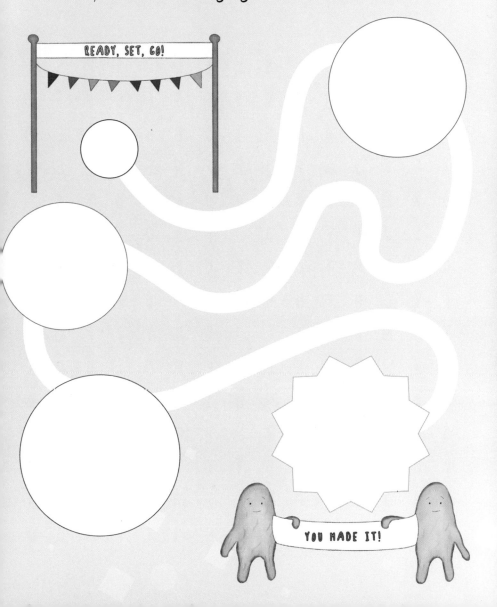

READY, SET, GO!

YOU MADE IT!

WHICH THREE EMPOWERING WORDS DO YOU SEE FIRST?

```
P  C  T  U  D  V  O  K  I  S  G  S  P  S  T
X  I  M  R  J  Z  R  S  E  S  E  G  O  S  R
H  W  H  C  O  N  F  I  D  E  N  T  S  E  A
I  E  C  S  N  F  J  B  F  N  E  P  I  C  V
O  P  A  E  D  P  M  F  V  I  H  U  T  C  E
C  S  V  L  E  N  O  O  E  P  Q  T  I  U  L
G  O  I  A  T  C  E  R  C  P  X  P  V  S  L
L  R  C  U  F  H  U  I  V  A  U  E  E  W  L
T  E  A  P  M  T  C  J  R  H  Y  P  P  A  H
M  H  W  T  N  H  O  P  E  F  A  R  U  Q  I
K  R  G  E  E  F  A  M  I  L  Y  G  S  R  R
G  O  V  I  V  F  B  V  Z  G  H  V  K  N  C
P  D  Y  B  L  Z  U  T  K  T  B  D  O  B  B
A  O  Q  Q  M  F  B  L  E  T  N  G  O  W  X
M  O  D  E  E  R  F  R  N  A  F  T  B  H  W
```

Use those three words to describe the day you want to have tomorrow. Write as many sentences as you need. (And finish the puzzle if you like! There are 20 encouraging words hiding in there, ready to shape your day!)

_____

_____

_____

_____

_____

_____

_____

_____

_____

_____

_____

_____

_____

COPING STRATEGY: GETTING GROUNDED

Reset an anxious mind by using your five senses to ground yourself in the moment.

5 things I can see _____

_____

_____

4 things I can touch _____

_____

_____

3 things I can hear _____

_____

_____

2 things I can smell _____

_____

_____

1 thing I can taste

Ahhhh

_____

WHAT IN NATURE BRINGS YOU PEACE?

IMAGINE...

The sound of a gentle afternoon rain.

A clear night sky filled with stars.

The rumbling of a distant thunderstorm.

Walking on freshly fallen snow.

Birdsong at sunrise.

The vibrant colors of a summer sunset.

Golden leaves rustling in the breeze.

On each leaf, write something you want
to "leaf" behind to feel more at peace.
Feel free to draw more leaves!

Make this page your vision board. Cut and paste, draw or jot down the images, quotations and other musings that inspire you to want to be your best self.

Did you know that pleasant, temporary distraction
is a valid way of coping with anxiety? It gives your brain
a chance to rest and recover. What are 10 things
that bring you comfort and happiness?

BINGING YOUR FAVORITE TV SHOWS CAN BE THERAPEUTIC.

1 _____

2 _____

3 _____

4 _____

5 _____

6 _____

7 _____

8 _____

9 _____

10 _____

QUICK! In five seconds, underline what you value most.

beauty * caring * other people * friendship * loyalty * love * forgiveness * money * success * health * freedom * generosity * confidence * perspective * honesty * knowledge * integrity * skills * admiration * silence * comfort * desire * power * ambition * hope * music * fashion * fame * culture * humility * laughter * family * pride * confidence * pleasure * company * nature * respect * travel * creativity * change * comfort * praise * rest * ambition * selflessness * patience * gratitude * humor

NOW GO BACK AND CIRCLE WHAT YOU MISSED.

When you love someone, you accept them for who they are. What do you need to accept about yourself so you can love yourself better?

_____

_____

_____

_____

_____

_____

_____

_____

_____

I am a magnificent lump of weirdness!

Write down the positive affirmations you need today on each wave and let those calming thoughts wash over you.

You've made it through another day,
Anxiety Blob! Be proud of yourself.

HOW MIGHT YOU REWARD YOURSELF?

1 ....

2 ....

3 ....

4 ....

5 ....

6 ....

7 ....

8 ....

9 ....

10 ....

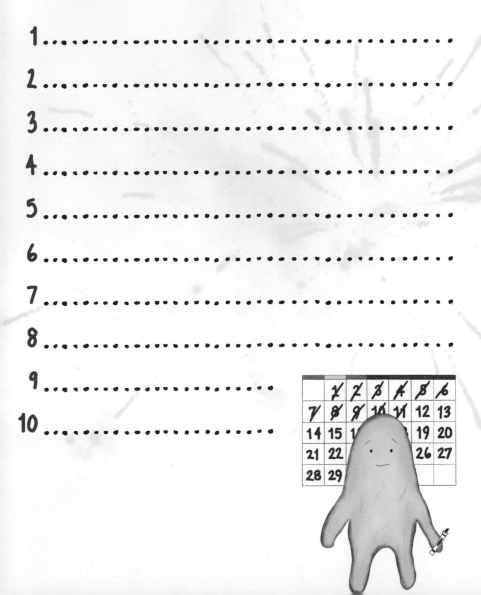

RATE YOUR ANXIETY LEVEL TODAY.

What can you do today to lower your anxiety by one point?

AAHHHH!!

10

9

8

7

6

5

4

3

2

1 Ahhh.

What's your inner critic trying to direct your attention to today? Imagine you could invite them over for coffee and let them vent. How do you think this misguided voice might be trying to help you?

(THEY MEAN WELL.)

This is a page to do as you please—whether that's checking in with yourself, doodling to your heart's content or making a to-do list. Do whatever feels comfortable, Anxiety Blob.

Imagine you could wake up tomorrow and live the rest of your life anxiety-free. That's right — no more crippling fear of failure, executive dysfunction, worst-case scenario planning, etc. What would you gain? But what would you lose? Why is it OK to experience anxiety from time to time, Anxiety Blob?

_____

_____

_____

_____

_____

_____

_____

_____

Anxiety and insomnia often go hand in hand.

There may be a medical component if your sleep is severely impacted, so check with your doctor. At night, your brain is tired and less able to regulate, which makes it easier for the anxiety-inducing thoughts to get in. What are three reassuring statements you can repeat to yourself to quiet your mind? (Ex. "I am safe." "I am loved." "Tomorrow there will be coffee.") If it helps, imagine you are reassuring someone else. What would you say to them?

_____

_____

_____

_____

_____

_____

I will be OK.
Most likely.

_____

_____

_____

_____

_____

_____

As soon as I make it through my
to-do list tomorrow, I'm going to:

* build the biggest, comfiest
    pillow fort ever

* give myself a sweet treat

* sink into a relaxing bath

* take a soothing walk around my
    neighborhood

* curl up and binge my favorite
    TV series

* spend time doing a hobby I love

* ALL of the above!

BREATHING EXERCISE

Feeling anxious? Try this:

* Exhale deeply.

* Hold for a second or two.

* Now inhale slowly through your nose for four seconds, filling up as much of your lungs as you can.

* Hold your breath for seven seconds, then slowly exhale through your mouth for eight seconds.

* Repeat three times.

How do you feel?

ANXIETY ATTACKS ARE THE WORST.

It's important to be gentle with yourself in the aftermath, because your whole body has just experienced a traumatic event. What would you say to someone who is going through one? What encouragement would you offer?

You survived! I'm proud of you.

Take five minutes and get comfy.

Let yourself breathe. Outside of your work, your family or any other commitments you've made, you are a person with hopes, dreams and talents.

Fill in each petal with what makes you unique.

For some Anxiety Blobs, self-acceptance takes time and practice. Look at your reflection in a mirror today and say three kind things about yourself out loud, whether it's about how you look or who you are. If this proves difficult for you, describe your experience below. If you were able to do it, describe how you want to appreciate and empower others today. Make a habit of looking for the good in people — that means you, too!

Meditation is a great tool we can use to practice emotionally disconnecting from our thoughts. After all, no matter what life throws at us, we can learn to be less reactive. Understanding how we process information is just as important.

WHAT ARE YOU THANKFUL FOR IN THIS MOMENT?

* Take a few deep breaths and focus on breathing in and breathing out.

* Draw your attention to the feeling of your lungs filling with air.

* Whatever thoughts arise, rather than block or ignore them, try to imagine them as passing clouds—neither good nor bad, simply there—and then gone.

(If you can only do this for a minute or a few seconds, that's OK.)

WHERE DID YOUR MIND GO? HOW DO YOU FEEL?

THINGS I NEED FOR TODAY:

* a cup of fresh, delicious coffee

* personal space

* a three-hour nap

* enchanted forest critters
  to clean my house

* alright, probably more coffee

* a notice congratulating me on
  winning the lottery

* a negativity-repelling force field

* aliens to take me back to
  my home planet

Beam
me up!

It's okay to tell your anxiety to $#*&! off.

Compartmentalizing until you have time to process is totally okay. You have things to do, so maybe just plan on a nice shower-cry later. What do you want to say to your anxiety when it's pestering you? NSFW language is fine.

_____

_____

_____

_____

_____

_____

_____

_____

_____

_____

_____

_____

_____

_____

Take a moment to remember how you've made it through each and every day of your life, all the way to this very moment. Yay you! Consider all the things you've overcome. Pay special attention to the things you once thought were impossible. What happened? What changed? And how have you changed, Anxiety Blob?

Make your own Anxiety Blob! Cut them out and give them a home wherever you like.

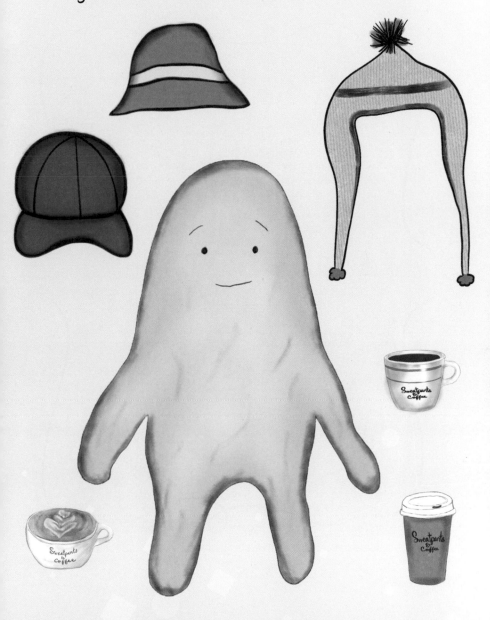

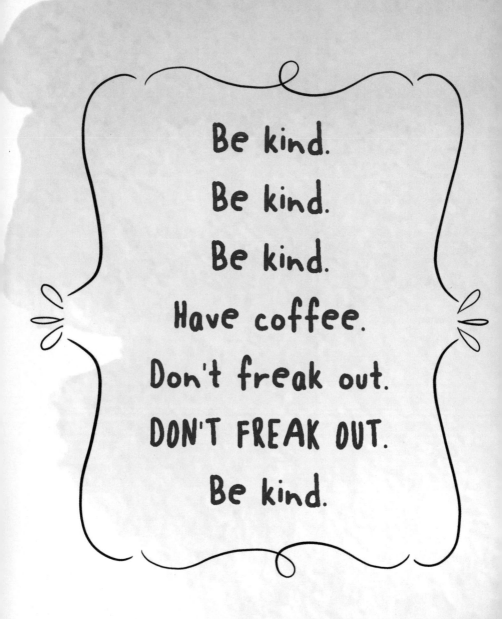

Describe a random act of kindness that someone performed for you. How were you affected?

What are five tangible ways you can show kindness to others?

· ·

· ·

· ·

· ·

· ·

· ·

· ·

· ·

· ·

· ·

Just because

Meditate on how your day went today (or yesterday). Did you land any great jokes? Did you speak from a place of kindness? Write down your takeaways, good or bad, and reflect on how you'd like tomorrow to go.

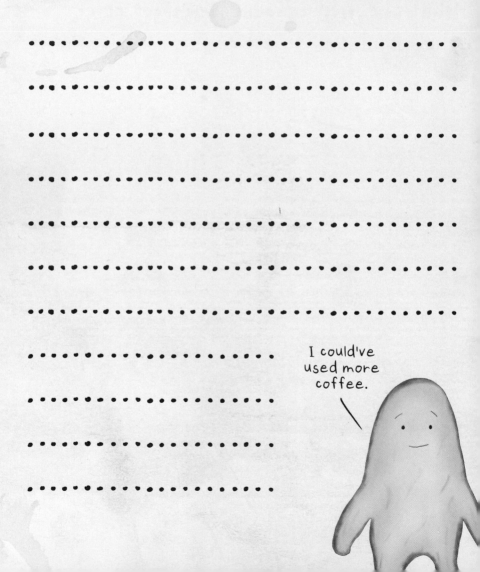

I could've used more coffee.

Rest is self-care.

Doing something you enjoy is self-care.

Practicing gratitude is self-care.

Asking to be left alone while
you enjoy your coffee is self-care.

TAKE GOOD CARE OF YOURSELF TODAY.

ANXIETY BLOBS ARE OFTEN EXTREMELY SELF-CONSCIOUS.

We compare ourselves to others and are convinced we fall short. But that's only because we're looking at ourselves through our anxiety goggles, and we aren't seeing clearly. It helps to have some pre-planned responses at the ready when the unkind, self-critical voices get loud. Write down three things you can say to yourself when you start feeling the urge to compare.

1 _____

_____

_____

2 _____

_____

_____

3 _____

_____

_____

Think of a fictional character you love.

Why do you love them? What qualities of theirs do you admire? What are two qualities you like about yourself, and what are two qualities you'd like to nurture in yourself? Playfulness? Creativity? Assertiveness? **No wrong answers here.**

_____

_____

_____

_____

_____

_____

_____

_____

_____

DRAW THE TASTIEST THING YOU ATE THIS WEEK.

WEEKEND GOALS

REST. RELAX.
RECHARGE.
RE-CAFFEINATE.
TWITCH BETWEEN
DIMENSIONS
AND VISIT
MAGICAL REALMS.
NAP?

Go outside, if only for a few minutes, and doodle what you see.

Vague worries can swirl around in your head like a swarm of bees. It helps to name them. **What are three specific worries that are buzzing in your brain?** They can be huge or tiny.

1 _____

2 _____

3 _____

Write down the thoughts that go with these worries. Remember, your feelings are real, but your anxiety may give you thoughts that are incorrect. Do these thoughts make sense? For each worry, ask yourself, "Is there an action to be taken?" If yes, what can you reasonably do, taking into account where you currently are, physically and mentally? If there is nothing to be done at this time, imagine setting that worry down. You can leave it here, on this page and come back for it later.

1 _____

_____

_____

_____

2 _____

_____

_____

_____

3 _____

_____

_____

_____

WAYS TO TEND TO YOUR MENTAL HEALTH

✳ Get enough rest

✳ Feed yourself

✳ Take your meds if you need to

✳ Allow space for your emotions

✳ Text a friend

✳ See a professional if necessary

✳ Be creative; find ways to express yourself

✳ Make sure your boundaries are strong

✳ Check in with yourself frequently

✳ Suspend judgement of yourself

✳ Acknowledge the truth of your experience

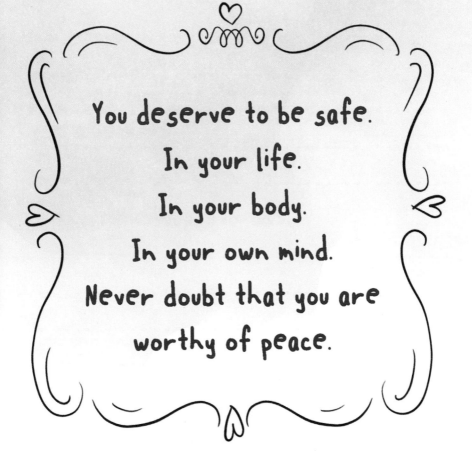

You deserve to be safe.
In your life.
In your body.
In your own mind.
Never doubt that you are
worthy of peace.

You deserve goodness, you dear
Anxiety Blob. Imagine yourself
happy, calm and fulfilled.

What does that look like?

· ·

· ·

· ·

· ·

Where are you?

· ·

· ·

· ·

· ·

What are you doing?

· ·

· ·

· ·

· ·

Think about what makes you
feel happy and at peace.
Name your favorite calming...

COLOR _____

SONG _____

PLACE _____

SOUND _____

ACTIVITY _____

Life can be strange and unpredictable and hard. All we can do is figure it out as we go. You know how to do this because you've been doing it your whole life. **What are three strategies you use to stay centered?** If you aren't currently using any strategies, make one up! Make it achievable — something you know is doable for you. Be proud that you're here and trying.

1..

....

....

2..

....

....

3..

....

....

Do you encourage and support yourself the way you encourage and support others?

If not, maybe at some point you decided that your needs don't matter. It's time to unlearn that, beloved one.

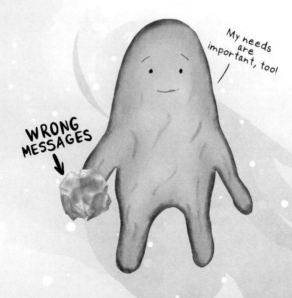

Your brain is always listening, and it responds to your internal monologue, or dialogue, or multi-character stage production—whatever is going on in your head.
It believes what you tell it. Write down five crappy things you say to yourself. Beneath that, write out five loving things you need to hear. Read them over. Practice saying them to yourself (silently is fine). This may feel squirmy at first, but stay with it, you anxious, brave butternut squash.

5 CRAPPY THINGS

5 LOVING THINGS

IT HELPS TO LET SECRET ANXIETIES BREATHE.

Bring them out into the light and air.
What's something you've been lugging around
in your mental backpack? Take that thing out of
the bag and make room for some "in case
of freak out" supplies. Patience, chocolate,
self-love, meds, whatever.

What are seven things you'd put in your support bag?

1. _____
2. _____
3. _____
4. _____
5. _____
6. _____
7. _____

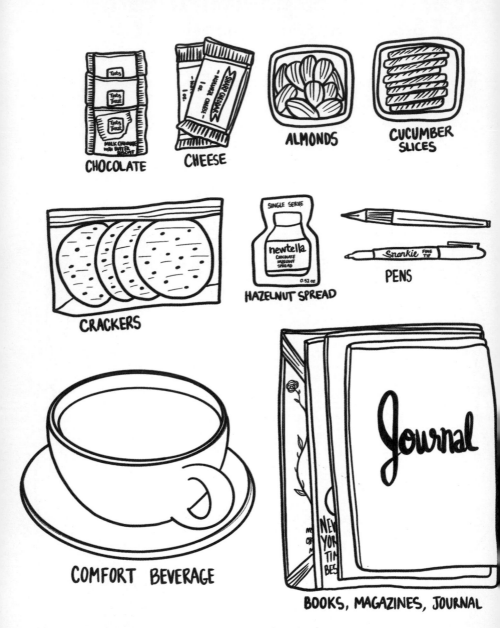

CHOCOLATE

CHEESE

ALMONDS

CUCUMBER SLICES

CRACKERS

HAZELNUT SPREAD

PENS

COMFORT BEVERAGE

BOOKS, MAGAZINES, JOURNAL

IN CASE YOU NEED TO SEE THIS
▽▽▽▽▽▽▽▽▽▽▽▽▽▽▽▽▽▽▽

Be kind to yourself.

You did the best
you could at the time.

You're doing your best now.

You don't have to have a plan.

Just keep on being here.

Good job still
being here!

Dealing with anxiety and intrusive thoughts DOES NOT make you weak. You're still here, and that's amazing. List 10 things you are able to do despite your anxiety or other challenges. Celebrate them like a kindergarten drawing you'd tape to the fridge.

1 _____

2 _____

3 _____

4 _____

5 _____

6 _____

7 _____

8 _____

9 _____

10 _____

Avoidance is a symptom of anxiety.

This is your brain trying to protect you from an unpleasant or stressful experience. But decisions made from a place of fear prevent you from living intentionally.

What's something you know you've been avoiding? No shame. You're just acknowledging what's going on with you.

What are three small steps you can take to help yourself move forward?

If I ignore it, maybe it'll go away.

1 . . . .

. . . .

. . . .

2 . . . .

. . . .

. . . .

3 . . . .

. . . .

. . . .

USE THIS PAGE TO JOT DOWN YOUR TO-DO LIST TODAY OR GIVE YOURSELF A FEW WORDS OF ENCOURAGEMENT. YOU GOT THIS.

GROWTH IS NOT GRACEFUL.

IT'S STRETCHING, AND BREAKING THROUGH,
AND DISCOMFORT.

IT'S DIGGING UP ROOTS AND TAKING WRONG
TURNS AND MESSING UP SPECTACULARLY.

IT'S STITCHING YOURSELF TOGETHER INTO
SOMETHING NEW BUT SOMEHOW MORE YOU.

AND IT'S WORTH IT.

Remember that your beautiful, imperfect self is enough. All you can ever do is the best you can do.

What did you do well today? What are you looking forward to doing better tomorrow?

· ·

· ·

· ·

· ·

· ·

· ·

· ·

· ·

You have the chance to write a letter to someone you know telling them something you haven't been able to say, with a guaranteed positive reaction in return. You don't have to actually say it to them (but you can!).
Write it out here, just to clarify your thoughts.

_____

_____

_____

_____

_____

_____

_____

_____

_____

_____

_____

_____

_____

_____

One way to make significant changes feel more manageable is to break them down into smaller pieces. List three changes you'd like to make. Beneath each one, list three tiny steps that will move you closer to that goal. Make them realistic.

BIG SCARY CHANGE
↓
small doable steps
1. _____
2. _____
3. _____

1 . . . .

. . . .

. . . .

. . . .

2 . . . .

. . . .

. . . .

. . . .

3 . . . .

. . . .

. . . .

. . . .

There are days, maybe weeks and months, when it feels like you are never going to move forward.

When you doubt yourself because you can't see any progress.

But the truth is, if you're waking up every day and doing the hard, beautiful, necessary work of living and learning, you ARE growing. It's impossible not to. So, keep going.

When you need a page to angrily scribble all the things that have been bothering you, use this page. You can even tear it out if you like. It won't mind. That's why it's here.

Your imagination is powerful.

If you're an Anxiety Blob, that can be both a blessing and a curse. It's a blurse. You're great at imagining disaster scenarios, but — hear me out — what if everything doesn't go horribly? What if things go well? Or at least okay? Write down a future event that is worrying you. Next, beneath it, write about one incident that caused you great anxiety but worked out all right. Note to your anxious self: things can also turn out OK.

_____

_____

_____

_____

_____

_____

_____

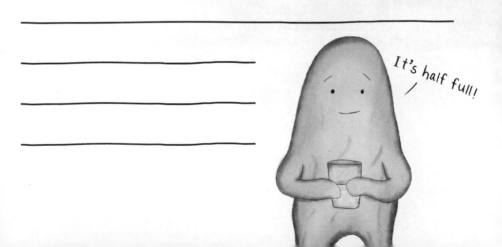

Draw a portrait of yourself using whatever
colors you like. Or patterns. Or words.
You contain multitudes, Anxiety Blob.
Show the world who you really are.

What are three things you want to believe about yourself? What changes could you make in order for each of these things to feel true? It's OK if it feels like a long journey. Framing these ideas with words is the first step.

....

....

....

....

....

....

....

....

....

Cultivate the habit
of finding joy
in small, ordinary things
and you will always have
light to see by.

Take a few minutes to reflect on your day, Anxiety Blob. Consider all the little things that went right. Say them out loud to yourself or draw them below. If today wasn't so great, write down what you hope will work out tomorrow.

If it brings you comfort, allow yourself to drink it in.

What are some happy surprises that happened to
you recently? Did you get a free latte? Did someone
hold the door for you? Did you find five bucks
in your pocket while doing the laundry?

LITTLE JOYS ADD UP. LIST THEM HERE!

_____

_____

_____

_____

_____

_____

_____

_____

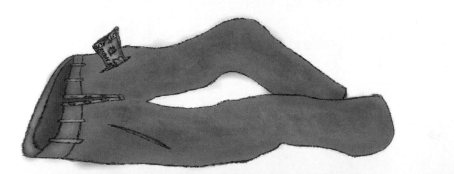

You can ask your future self any question you want. Anything. What would you want to know? Now remember:

YOU HAVE THE ANSWERS INSIDE YOU IF YOU LISTEN FOR THEM.

Imagine the energy your brain uses to overthink things as a source of power you could harness. What would it look like? Draw what you think your active mind could power if given the chance.

Kindness received can help you through a tough time and give you a much-needed shift in perspective. But kindness given can have an even more powerful effect. Describe a time when you were there for someone else and it ended up changing you. How were you different afterwards?

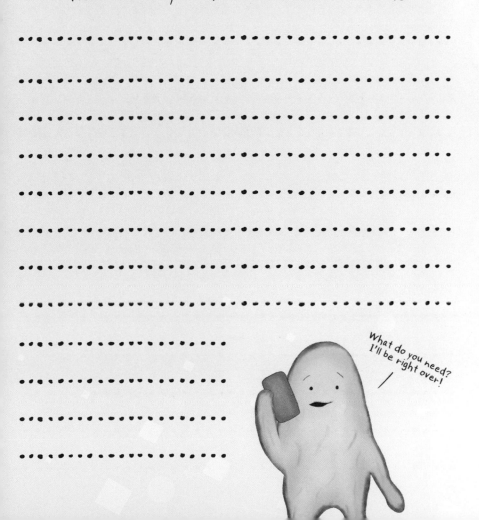

What do you need? I'll be right over!

Even on days when you feel exhausted and discouraged, there are reasons to be hopeful. You might have to squint to see them, but they're there. Start by listing three of them, and see if you can think of more.

1. ....

....

2. ....

....

3. ....

....

AND THAT'S NOT INCLUDING....

....

....

....

....

....

Draw an award for whatever you accomplished today. For example: maybe you got out of bed. Maybe you changed from pajamas to sweatpants and washed your face. There's a trophy for that! Anything goes! Bonus points for writing your acceptance speech.

DRINK GOOD COFFEE.
BE KIND. BE GRATEFUL.
NOTICE BEAUTY. BE UNAPOLOGETICALLY
JOYFUL AND WEIRD. LISTEN TO
YOUR HEART AND BELIEVE
WHAT IT TELLS YOU.
BE YOURSELF IN THE WORLD,
AS HONESTLY AS YOU CAN.

For Anxiety Blobs, it's important to develop the skill of asking for help. It's not easy, but you can do it. Call a hotline, text a friend, talk to someone you trust, send up a signal flare—you'll have to figure out what works best for you, and the way to do that is by trying. Reaching out can feel scary, but your well-being is always worth it.

Promise.

~~~~~~~~~~~~~~~~~~~~~~~~~~~~~~~~~

_____

_____

_____

_____

_____

_____

_____

_____

_____

The NAMI (National Alliance on Mental Illness) Helpline can be reached Monday through Friday, 10 am—6 pm, ET. 1-800-950-NAMI (6264) or info@nami.org

You're building the coziest, comfiest blanket fort for yourself. What's in it?

_____

_____

_____

_____

_____

_____

_____

_____

_____

_____

Part of taking responsibility for yourself is prioritizing your mental, emotional and physical health. Write down one thing you can do to support yourself in each of these areas. You may not always do a great job of this but make it a goal. Forgive yourself if you don't hit the mark and be sure to celebrate even partial successes. You are worthy of care, and the time you take to meet your own needs isn't selfish.

MENTAL HEALTH

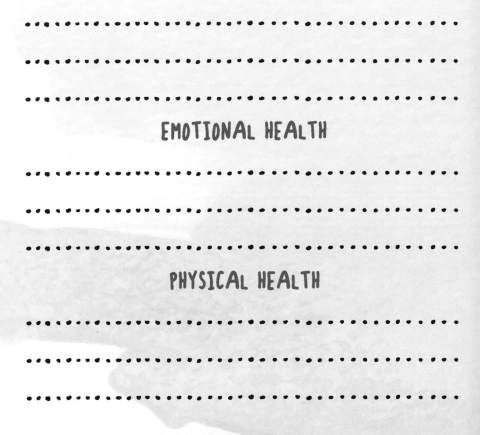

....

....

....

EMOTIONAL HEALTH

....

....

....

PHYSICAL HEALTH

....

....

....

Set a digital timer for 10 minutes,
then close your eyes and do absolutely
nothing until the timer goes off.
Let your mind wander wherever it
likes, then come back to this page
and describe where it went.

....

....

....

....

....

....

....

....

Fortify yourself with a soothing thought or your favorite comfort beverage, then take a tiny baby step out of your comfort zone. Circle four experiences (or hey, try them all!) and make a point to pencil in one of them each week for a month.

try a new restaurant

go for a hike

read a new book

see a concert

paint or draw something

visit a museum

take a weekend trip

watch a movie in the theater

meditate

try a new recipe

explore a farmers market

volunteer

buy a plant and keep it alive for more than four days

Anxiety can cause you to play and replay the highlight reel of your very worst mistakes until you feel paralyzed. But remember: you get things right more often than not. It may not come naturally, but try to cultivate the habit of noticing your mini-triumphs. What are 10 small successes you can celebrate? (Showering and feeding yourself are acceptable answers.)

MADE MISTAKES BUT ALSO DID LOTS OF STUFF RIGHT!

1. ....

2. ....

3. ....

4. ....

5. ....

6. ....

7. ....

8. ....

9. ....

10. ....

3 Things That Comforted Me Today

* _____

* _____

* _____

EVERYONE HAS A THEME SONG.

The one that makes you smile, crank up the volume, and maybe perform an impromptu lip-sync routine in the car. What's yours? How do you feel when you hear it? What other songs are on your feel-good playlist?

My theme song is... _____

_____

It makes me feel... _____

_____

_____

My alternate theme songs are... _____

_____

_____

One of the fun ways Anxiety Blobs react to stress is by catastrophizing. Anxiety tells us we will be better prepared if we can think of the very worst storyline that could possibly play out, so we'll know what to do when the zombie apocalypse finally arrives.

The thing is, that's exhausting. These thoughts are the product of your brilliant but perhaps overactive mind. Write about one calamity you imagined that never actually happened.

REMEMBER: WORRIES ARE NOT PROPHECIES.

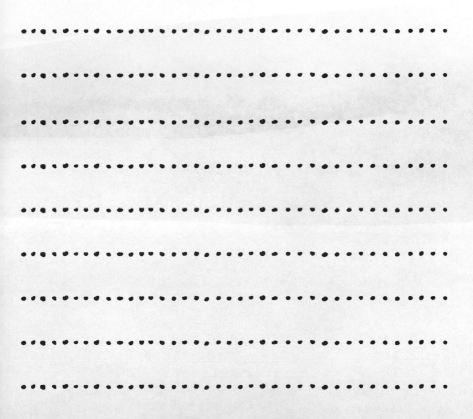

Get lost in a story.
Savor a peaceful moment
as it is unfolding.
Refresh your spirit
with what fascinates
and delights you.
Tending to your well-being
is sacred work.

Imagine your most recent successes, then draw them as headlines in a newspaper all about you. Maybe you nailed your latest project at work; maybe you remembered to buy more coffee at the store before you ran fresh out. What's the latest scoop on the story of your life?

One way to shift from anxiety to calm is to take a moment to recognize the things, big and small, that bring you joy. Set a timer for five minutes and see how many you can list.

When you feel anxious, you can end up time-traveling. Meaning, you're constantly off in the future, anticipating some imagined calamity, or you're looking back at the past, which cannot be changed but can still make you cringe. Gratitude anchors you to the present.

WHAT ARE YOU THANKFUL FOR IN THIS MOMENT?

....

....

....

....

....

....

....

....

STORIES ARE SELF-CARE.

They transport us to a different place and
allow our brains to rest and play.
What are three books you absolutely love?
Who are your favorite characters in each?
If books aren't your bag, feel free to
start with a TV series or favorite film.

1 _____

_____

2 _____

_____

3 _____

_____

Nothing like relaxing with a good book.

Sweatpants Coffee

Draw whatever you like without lifting
your pen or pencil from the page.
See what emerges.

You have been crushed into dust.
And you've had to reassemble
yourself so many times.
Tired, determined, wiser, different.
And each time, you learned
how to build yourself back up
with your two hands and your beating heart.
You are a wonder.

Think of three things you'd love to do.
Are you working on any of them now?
What are some small ways you could get started?

1 _____

_____

_____

2 _____

_____

_____

_____

3 _____

_____ Goals

_____

One step at
a time!

_____

WRITE ABOUT YOUR NON-NEGOTIABLES IN LIFE:

your priorities and needs. The more specific, the better. When you feel lost or confused about what you want or where you're headed, let yourself be guided by what you require in order to be healthy and happy.

What's the worst unsolicited advice you've ever received about dealing with your anxiety? What would you have rather heard?

....

....

....

....

....

....

....

....

....

....

Draw the people or places that have made a lasting impact on your life in wonderful ways.

We are all linked by our common experience of being humans on this planet, together. But that doesn't prevent us from feeling lonely, especially if we have anxiety about forming or maintaining relationships with others. We need connection, though, in whatever form we can manage, whether in person, over text, online, tin cans with string, etc. What works best for you? Why? What is one way you'll try to connect this week?

_____

_____

_____

_____

_____

_____

_____

_____

_____

_____

_____

I love my computer friends.

Use this page to check in with yourself.
How's your anxiety management coming along
today, this week or even this month?
Draw or write down your progress here.

Or do none of the above and fill this page
with a bunch of shapes. We won't tell.

When you're in a dark and difficult place, it's easy to forget that feelings aren't forever. They DO pass. Imagine your kindest, wisest self has come to sit with you. What would this version of you say to the you who is struggling?

What are a few of your
favorite soothing activities?
Why do you think they help you
feel more at peace?

_____

_____

_____

_____

_____

_____

_____

_____

FILL IN THE DIRECTIONS SURROUNDING THIS COMPASS WITH SOMETHING THAT...

North ... inspires you.

East ... brings you comfort.

South ... you hope to leave behind.

West ... you're proud of.

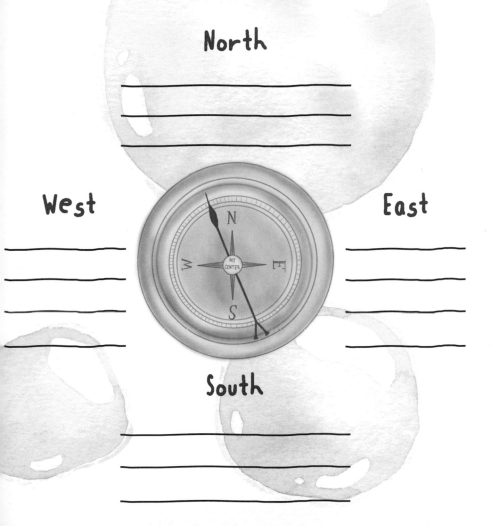

North

_____

_____

_____

West

_____

_____

_____

East

_____

_____

_____

South

_____

_____

_____

DRAW SOMETHING—MATERIAL OR OTHERWISE—YOU RECENTLY GAVE SOMEONE.

Think of a happy memory.

It can be a small, ordinary moment.
Allow yourself to revisit this feeling. What do you notice?
What are your surroundings? Are you with anyone?
What are you doing (or not doing)?
Carry this memory with you, always.
How can you find ways to access this place inside you?

Wow!

SOME MOMENTS YOU SAVOR.
OTHERS YOU ENDURE.

And here's the thing:
You are as alive and valid
in the second kind of moment
as you are in the first.
Don't let anyone
tell you differently.

Every time you are able to say no and mean it, you make space in your life for more of what you really want and need. It takes practice to get good at this but remind yourself that solid boundaries will allow you to feel less resentful and to operate from a place of wholeness and compassion. What is one thing you'd like to say no to? Write down what you want to say. Be specific and direct. Don't overexplain or apologize. You might be shaky at first, but you'll get better each time.

_____

_____

_____

_____

_____

_____

_____

_____

_____

_____

_____

Anxiety doesn't always make sense but the fact that it isn't logical doesn't mean your experience isn't real or valid. What are some nonsensical anxieties you have? It's okay if they're utterly absurd.

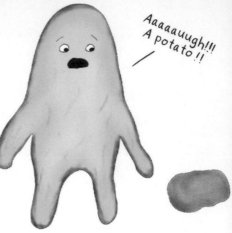

Aaaaauugh!!! A potato!!

· ·

· ·

· ·

· ·

· ·

· ·

· ·

· ·

· ·

· ·

Doodle the three things you can't live without.
Did someone you love give them to you?
How do they bring you comfort?

When we are in fear, it's hard to be loving.
We can be reactive or closed off. We might say or do
things we don't mean, especially to ourselves.
But the truth is that this is when we most
need patience. What are three ways you can be
kind to yourself when you're afraid?

1_____

_____

_____

2_____

_____

_____

3_____

_____

_____

You are doing such a great job of continuing to be here. You don't even need to know the big "why." What matters is that you are showing up for yourself, as best you can, and living your life. And simply by doing that, you've made the world a better, richer place. What do you see for yourself in a hopeful future? If you can't see it yet, go ahead and make something up. Get wild. Spaceships and wizards aren't off the table. Remember: **a vision has to start somewhere.**

_____

_____

_____

_____

_____

_____

_____

_____

_____

_____

_____

Explore three emotions you had today. When did you experience them? Describe one thought that accompanied each emotion.

1 ....
....
....

2 ....
....
....

3 ....
....
....

Take a breath and celebrate the fact that
you have carried the child you once were across time
to this moment. That's a BIG deal. Looking back,
what would you say to your younger self?

~~~~~~~~~~~~~~~~~~~~~~~~~~~~~~

_____

_____

_____

_____

_____

_____

_____

_____

You are
going
to make
it ♥

Use this page to check in with yourself today. How are you feeling?

What do I need today?

More often than not, Anxiety Blobs find themselves worrying about their interactions with other people. It can be so awkward!

Certain encounters that worry me:

_____

_____

_____

_____

I survive, though! And I'm learning every day. Whenever I think about these things, here's how I'll reframe them:

_____

_____

I can do difficult things.
Like reaching out
when I need connection.

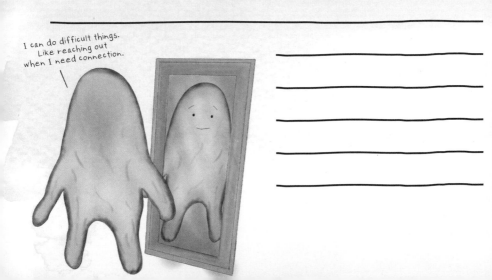

_____

_____

_____

_____

_____

MORNING PROCESS:

1. Make coffee.

2. Drink coffee.

3. Face the day!

4. Realize the day is also facing you and now it's weird.

5. Turn around. Have more coffee until you think of a way to excuse yourself without arousing suspicion.

Identifying anxiety triggers is helpful
when developing coping strategies.
What are three of your triggers? It's OK if you
don't know what to do about them.
For now, simply acknowledge that they are real.

1 ....
....
....

2 ....
....
....

3 ....
....
....

Unexpected
small talk!
ACK

FILL THIS PAGE WITH YOUR FAVORITE MOTIVATIONAL WORDS OR QUOTES.

FOR SOME ANXIETY BLOBS, SUNDAYS CAN BE EXTRA ROUGH.

What are three things you can do during the week that will make your Sunday (and impending week) less stressful?

1 _____

_____

_____

2 _____

_____

_____

3 _____

_____

_____

Who you are and how you feel are two separate things! Finish the "I am" sentences with a few different feelings on your plate today, then go back and see how you can reframe them. **This too shall pass, Anxiety Blob.**

I am_____.
Actually, I feel_____
because _____
_____.

I am_____.
Actually, I feel_____
because _____
_____.

I am_____.
Actually, I feel_____
because _____
_____.

Feelings aren't forever!

NAME FIVE THINGS YOU THINK ARE YOUR STRENGTHS.

Any five. No power is too weird or inconsequential. These qualities are what make you YOU. Focus on character traits, like thoughtfulness, empathy or honesty.

1..

2..

3..

4..

5..

TRY TO REMEMBER THAT LIFE IS A SERIES
OF PASSING MOMENTS. EVEN YOUR VERY WORST
FREAKOUT OR HEARTBREAK IS MADE UP OF THEM.
THIS MOMENT IS SURVIVABLE.
AND BREATH BY BREATH, SECOND BY SECOND,
YOUR UNIVERSE IS CONSTANTLY REMAKING ITSELF.

Anxiety and depression (or any other struggle) can make you feel utterly alone. It SUCKS. But here are some things to remember:

* No matter what, there's always someone in your corner: you.

* There are others who are experiencing what you are feeling, and even if you don't know them, you are connected.

* You are allowed to ask for and accept help.

What are three manageable actions you can take on your own behalf, when you're ready?

1...
....

2...
....

3...
....

Draw a detailed, Expressionist portrait
of the last time your anxiety led you to go out
of your way to help someone else.

JUST KIDDING!

Draw any animal. (Seriously. Any animal. Maybe a cat?
Or a red panda. Or a wallaby. Whatever you want!)

For Anxiety Blobs, fear can be the tension between what we want/need and the desire to be safe. Identifying your fears can help you understand the specific kind of safety you crave. And once you begin to understand that, you'll be on the path to stepping out from under those fears and allowing yourself to experience new things.

SO GET IT ALL OUT. WHAT ARE YOU AFRAID OF?

Failure can be a wonderful teacher. Think back to three times you thought you failed. Remember: all this means is you've figured out what doesn't work, and that you are a learning model of human.

WHAT LESSONS CAN YOU TAKE FROM THOSE EXPERIENCES?

1..

....

....

2..

....

....

3..

....

....

I made a mistake but I learned from it

List **ALL** the things you associate with each of the following words:

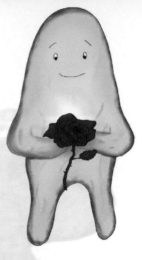

JOY

LAUGHTER

PEACE

HOPE

COURAGE

Pick three traits you would like others to see in you.

1 ....

2 ....

3 ....

WHAT CAN YOU DO TO SHOW THOSE TRAITS MORE OVERTLY?

....

....

....

....

....

....

....

....

List the top five things you say to yourself
every day. (Are those kind things?
What would you rather say to yourself?)

1 ....

....

2 ....

....

3 ....

....

4 ....

....

5 ....

....

Whatever happens today,
I will remember that I am enough!

What if, instead of imagining exactly how terrible something will be, you anticipate the possibility of... how great it COULD be? You deserve goodness, and it's seeking you, right now. Create your own inescapable joy movie trailer tag line!

EXAMPLE:
* Happiness inches closer. Resistance is futile.
* I will achieve my dreams. The quest begins!

* ....

* ....

* ....

* ....

* ....

* ....

* ....

* ....

* ....

PICK TWO LONG-TERM GOALS FOR YOURSELF.

Describe which first steps you can take to turn those dreams into reality.

In it for the long haul!

LIFE

START

_____

_____

_____

_____

_____

_____

_____

_____

DRAW YOUR VERY OWN BLANKET FORT.
Give your Anxiety Blob the plush palace of your dreams!

TRY NOT TO COMPARE YOUR STRUGGLE
TO ANYONE ELSE'S. AND ESPECIALLY DON'T
THINK OTHER PEOPLE HAVE IT WORSE.

HARD IS JUST HARD.

IT'S OK TO ACKNOWLEDGE THAT.

HAVE YOU GIVEN YOURSELF A BREAK LATELY?

When was the last time you took a day or even an hour off to do what you love in peace?
List three things you've been meaning to do. Now's the time to replenish yourself!

BE
BACK
LATER

* _____
  _____

* _____
  _____

* _____
  _____

Save this page for a day when you need
an unstructured space to relax.
Fill it with soothing things or take in its
unencumbered glory while you meditate.

Write out five anxious thoughts that have been bothering you, then write five affirmations to help put those thoughts in perspective. You don't even have to fully believe them right now — just get them down on paper. You can always come back to this page later.

ANXIOUS THOUGHT	AFFIRMATION
e.g. What if I don't finish my to-do list today?	I will take things one step at a time.
1	
2	
3	
4	
5	

THIS PAGE IS YOUR MOMENT OF ZEN.

Doodle, bullet journal or scribble as you like. Just do it peacefully.

Name three things you've learned,
either from experience or from
teacher figures in your life. How do you
think your life has benefited?

1 ....

....

....

....

2 ....

....

....

....

3 ....

....

....

....

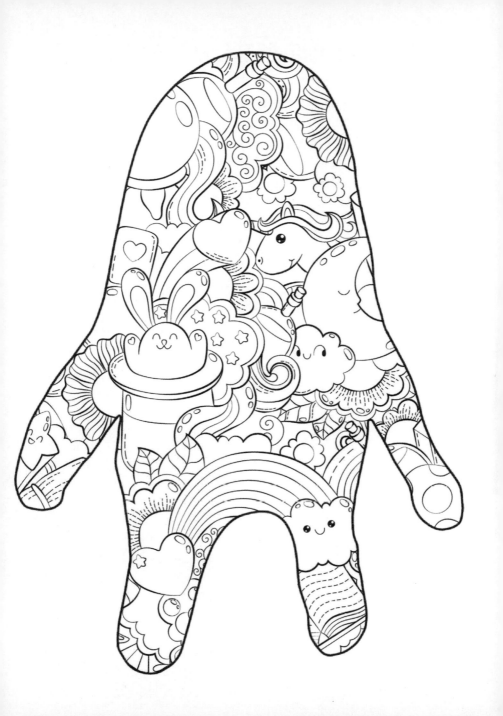

SETTING BOUNDARIES TAKES PRACTICE.

If you've been overextending yourself lately and feeling depleted, physically and/or emotionally, describe how you're going to prioritize your own needs this week.

_____

_____

_____

_____

_____

_____

_____

_____

_____

_____

_____

_____

What's your favorite time of day?
Why? How do you feel then?

It's no secret anxiety distorts the way we Anxiety Blobs see the world. Try putting on your compassion glasses. Look at yourself through them. What are three kind things you can tell yourself to get through a hard moment?

✳ ....

....

....

✳ ....

....

....

✳ ....

....

....

Whoahhhh.

COMPASSION

Name five things you know you do well, big or small.

EVERYONE'S GOOD AT SOMETHING!

1 _____

_____

2 _____

_____

3 _____

_____

4 _____

_____

5 _____

_____

Name your top five favorite things to do
at the end of the week.
How can you engage in these activities even
(especially!) when life is hectic? Next to each activity,
write down when and where you'll do them.

Sometimes it can be hard to separate what we want from what we need. Name five things you've wanted (to have or achieve), then describe how you think things will be different once you have them.

What does your community of kindred spirits look like? Do you see them in person, or do you chat online? It's OK if you don't feel like you have a community right now. You'll find them. Start by figuring out what works for you.

List three ways you are comfortable connecting with others.

1 _____

_____

2 _____

_____

3 _____

_____

Smells activate the amygdala and hippocampus—big words for the parts of the brain associated with emotion and memory. What are some of your favorites? List them here along with the feelings or memories they evoke.

ANXIETY ISN'T ALL IN YOUR MIND.

The brain is an organ that sends signals throughout the body. What are some ways your anxiety manifests physically?

. . . .

. . . .

. . . .

. . . .

. . . .

. . . .

. . . .

. . . .

. . . .

. . . .

. . . .

. . . .

. . . .

. . . .

LET YOURSELF BE SOFT FOR A MOMENT.
YOUR HEART, YOUR BREATH,
YOUR WORDS, YOUR THOUGHTS.
MAKE A SMALL, CLEAR SPACE
FOR YOUR BUSY MIND TO COME TO REST.
DISREGARD THE WORLD AND ITS DEMANDS,
JUST FOR A BIT. IT'LL STILL BE THERE
WHEN YOU'RE READY TO RE-ENGAGE.

Anxiety Blobs often take responsibility for things that do not belong to us, like other people's feelings or issues. What (or who) do you need to let go of in order to be happier?

. . . .

. . . .

. . . .

. . . .

. . . .

. . . .

. . . .

. . . .

. . . .

. . . .

. . . .

Draw your favorite place—real or imaginary. Or both.

Think back to three times someone praised or complimented you, whether it was something you were wearing, the thoughtful blog post you wrote or the fact that you showed up to their party because they understand your social anxiety is real. What did you do? How did their words make you feel? Sometimes, anxiety can cause discomfort in these situations or make you disbelieve what you're hearing. Challenge those thoughts and allow yourself to sit with the discomfort. Then simply say, "Thank you." Allow people to be good to you.

1. . . . .
. . . .
. . . .

2. . . . .
. . . .
. . . .

3. . . . .
. . . .
. . . .

YOU ARE BEAUTIFUL!

Um...thank you...

It's so easy to remember all the things that are
out of our control. (Thanks a lot, anxiety. We know.)
So right now, list all the things you can control.

* _____
* _____
* _____
* _____
* _____
* _____
* _____
* _____
* _____

Give because you want to.
Say no because you need to.
Accept help and kindness
because you deserve to.
And if you aren't getting
what you need from others,
be tender with yourself,
and remember, always,
that there is an entire
Universe within you.
YOU ARE WONDROUS.

ABOUT THE AUTHOR

Nanea Hoffman is the founder of Sweatpants & Coffee, a social media platform, online community and lifestyle brand focused on comfort, creativity, inspiration and fun. She launched SweatpantsAndCoffee.com in 2013 as a place to explore the joys of everyday life and to foster meaningful connection. An avid builder of blanket forts since childhood, her goal has been to make Sweatpants & Coffee the coziest corner of the Internet. She is also the creator of the Anxiety Blob, a physical representation of her own anxiety disorder, which has since become a beloved mental health mascot for people around the world. The Anxiety Blob is a reminder that you are not alone, and that you are more than your anxiety.

Want your own Anxiety Blob? Go to SweatpantsAndCoffee.com to find your newest friend!

ACKNOWLEDGEMENTS

Sweatpants & Coffee would not exist without my dear friends and amazing partners Jessica Hancock, Shandle Blaha, Emily Parker, Barbara Doyle and Tony Delgado. Thank you for putting up with me, providing much needed perspective and laughter, and for keeping the place running. You hold up this blanket fort. I am humbled by and grateful for the wonderful community of kindreds, writers and fans who believed in this dream and who helped to make it a reality. Last, but certainly not least, I thank my husband, Bob, who is the best person I know and who holds my hand every step of the way, and my children, Matthew and Samantha, who are my heart. "I love you every."

Media Lab Books
For inquiries, call 646-838-6637

Copyright 2020 Topix Media Lab

Published by Topix Media Lab
14 Wall Street, Suite 4B
New York, NY 10005

Manufactured in Singapore

ISBN-13: 978-1-948174-58-9
ISBN-10: 1-948174-58-8

CEO Tony Romando

Vice President & Publisher Phil Sexton
Senior Vice President of Sales & New Markets Tom Mifsud
Vice President of Retail Sales & Logistics Linda Greenblatt
Director of Finance Vandana Patel
Manufacturing Director Nancy Puskuldjian
Financial Analyst Matthew Quinn
Brand Marketing & Promotions Assistant Emily McBride

Chief Content Officer Jeff Ashworth
Director of Editorial Operations Courtney Kerrigan
Creative Director Steven Charny
Photo Director Dave Weiss
Executive Editor Tim Baker

Content Editor Juliana Sharaf
Art Director Susan Dazzo
Senior Editor Trevor Courneen
Designer Kelsey Payne
Copy Editor & Fact Checker Tara Sherman

Co-Founders Bob Lee, Tony Romando

Nanea Hoffman
Founder/Editor-in-Chief

All illustrations Nanea Hoffman. Additional art Shutterstock.